LIVING BOLDLY

LIVING BOLDLY

A 31-DAY DEVOTIONAL FOR YOUNG ADULTS

RICK THOMAS

LIVING BOLDLY:
A 31-Day Devotional for Young Adults

ISBN 978-1-966741-14-5

Rick Thomas

Edited by Sheron Wallace

Life Over Coffee
8595 Pelham Rd Ste 400 #406,
Greenville, SC 29615
LifeOverCoffee.com

For I know the plans I have for you, declares the LORD,
plans for welfare and not for evil, to give you a future
and a hope.
(Jeremiah 29:11)

For additional resources, visit
lifeovercoffee.com

Table of Contents

Dedication

Once upon a time, I was a teenager in jail at the end of my rope. Having someone to believe in me and willing to guide me would have made a difference. Externally, I was a bad kid, but I had dreams of a different kind. I hope this book will bring a modicum of hope and help to a generation looking for answers. You might say, these are things I have learned. I share them with you so you may live boldly for God's fame, your benefit, and the good of others.

Introduction

Life is full of questions—big ones like, "What's my purpose?" And smaller, everyday ones like, "How do I make the right choice?" As a young adult, you're navigating one of the most formative seasons of your life. Going from child to adult in a brief season is as astounding as it is demanding. These years are full of opportunities to grow, challenges to overcome, and decisions that will shape your future. Every adult is aware of the decisions they made in their youth affected how they live today. Some would say, "If I could live my life over again, I would do things differently."

Fortunately, you have an opportunity before you to stave off future regret. This 31-day devotional is designed to help you explore what it means to live a life centered on God's truth. Each day is unique, offering practical wisdom rooted in Scripture, guiding you to think biblically about topics like relationships, identity, decision-making, and faith. These devotions aren't just about reading something hope-filled and inspirational; they're about reflecting, praying, and taking actionable steps toward living a Christ-centered life.

God's Word provides everything you need for life and godliness (2 Peter 1:3). Whether you're experiencing joy or struggling with doubt, His truth will guide and sustain you. I hope that this devotional will help you see God's hand in your life, understand His heart for you, and inspire you to glorify Him in all you do. I encourage you to share your reflections and plans with a close friend. Let the Hebrews writer's admonition be your motivation:

> And let us consider how to stir up one another to love and good works (Hebrews 10:24).

To stir up is to agitate or irritate. May the sweet Spirit of God bring the appropriate agitation in your life to stir you up to love and good works. Furthermore, may you imitate Him by becoming a biblical irritant to your friends.

Let's live boldly, seeking to know God more deeply and live for Him more fully.

Rick

Day 1

Embracing a God-Centered Life

As you embark on this 31-day journey, consider six essential truths about life, God, and yourself. These truths are not just ideas to ponder but steps toward a more Christ-centered life. Pick the one that seems most challenging and make a plan to change. I share these with you in no particular order.

> For to this you have been called, because Christ also suffered for you, leaving you an example, so that you might follow in his steps.
>
> (1 Peter 2:21)

1. **NORMAL:** Life often feels unfair. There's a good chance you didn't get the life you dreamed of or expected. That's normal. We live in a broken world under the curse of sin—a curse you didn't cause and a world you didn't create. But God is not absent. He is actively working in the lives of those who trust Him. Will you trust His plan for your life, even when life seems disappointing? What would trust mean practically?
2. **VICTIM:** You face a choice every day: Will you play the victim card or the responsibility card? Blaming others for your problems is easy—we all know how

to do it, and—I suppose—we're all guilty of doing it. But when you live in a state of blame, you remain stuck in bitterness. To be a victim is to carry sin, whether it's your sin or others. God did not build us to carry sin perpetually. We have a gospel for that. Recognize your disappointments, then decide to let go and trust God to guide you into the next phase of your life.

3. **RESPONSIBLE:** Maturity requires taking responsibility for your life. This assumption means you must let go of past offenses and disappointments. Yes, others may have sinned against you, but holding onto resentment and unforgiveness will only hinder your growth. Will you step into maturity by choosing an attitude of forgiveness toward others and taking ownership of your walk with Christ?

4. **CHOOSE:** The Bible presents the ultimate question: "Is God's Word true or false?" If you believe it is untrue, then following its instructions won't make sense to you, and you won't follow them consistently. But if you believe it's true, you must surrender your preferences, align your life with Scripture, and trust God's ways over your own. There are two paths before you: follow God or follow something else. Choose wisely.

5. **HOPE:** Your best life is not found in chasing the world's ideas of success but in following God's Word. It may not be the life you envisioned, but it will be the life God designed for your good, the benefit of others, and His fame. Will you embrace His plan and the hope He offers, even when it differs from your expectations?

6. **OPPORTUNITY:** Every challenge is an opportunity to grow closer to Christ. What will you choose? What alternative path could be better than following

the One who created and loves you? Every second provides an opportunity before you, and you will step into it. Take this time to consider: "Is there any opportunity greater than submitting to God's Word and walking in His ways?" Take that next step for God's fame and your good.

Time to Reflect

1. Take a moment to think about these six truths. Which one seems the hardest for you to embrace? Maybe you struggle with trusting God's plan, letting go of past offenses, or fully submitting to the Bible's authority. Whatever it is, write it down.
2. Now, make a plan to turn that challenge into an opportunity. Ask God for wisdom and strength to change. Talk to a trusted mentor or friend who can hold you accountable. Then, take the first step today.

Let's live boldly, together trusting God to transform our lives, one step at a time.

Day 2

Responding to Unfairness

One of life's most challenging realities is unfairness. Perhaps you have heard someone say, "It's not fair!" in response to something disappointing. Maybe you have said it yourself. If so, your frustration is natural because fairness aligns with how we think things should work. However, the reality is that life hasn't been fair since Adam disobeyed God in the Garden of Eden (Genesis 3:8-14). Adam's fall unleashed sin and death into a world God originally designed to be perfect (Genesis 2:7-9). Ever since unfairness has been woven into the fabric of life (Romans 5:12).

> Moreover, I saw under the sun that in the place of justice, even there was wickedness, and in the place of righteousness, even there was wickedness. I said in my heart, God will judge the righteous and the wicked, for there is a time for every matter and for every work.
>
> (Ecclesiastes 3:16-17)

Why Life Isn't Fair

The unfairness we see around us isn't God's fault—it's a result of sin. Adam's rebellion didn't just affect him; it corrupted all of creation. Every person is born with a sinful nature (James 1:14-15), which means that all of us, without exception, take turns sinning against one another (Romans 3:23). Imperfect people do imperfect things in an imperfect world. This cycle will continue until Jesus returns to make everything perfect (Revelation 21:4).

I'm not suggesting you should condone unfairness. God doesn't. He is a God of justice, and so are we. However, pretending life can or should be fair will only lead to uninterrupted frustration and bitterness. It's like walking into a car wash and expecting to stay dry—it's unrealistic. Instead of demanding fairness, we must decide how to respond to life's inevitable disappointments, which brings us to an all-important question.

How Will You Respond?

When faced with unfairness, you have two options: respond sinfully or respond like Christ. Complaining, retaliating, or seeking revenge—only perpetuates the cycle of sin (Proverbs 14:12). On the other hand, responding with godliness breaks the cycle of sinful responses in our lives. Jesus taught us to turn the other cheek (Luke 6:29), trusting God to work all things for good (Romans 8:28).

Jesus Himself faced the ultimate unfairness. He lived a perfect life but suffered and died for sins He didn't commit. Yet, instead of lashing out, He entrusted Himself to God, who judges justly (1 Peter 2:21-25). If we follow His example, we can rise above life's unfairness and experience the peace that comes from trusting God. We can be victorious, even as we grieve the unfairness in our fallen world.

Practicing Godly Responses

Learning to respond well to unfair situations takes time and practice. But the more you choose to respond with humility, an attitude of forgiveness, and trust in God, the more you'll grow in Christlikeness. Over time, you'll find that life's unfairness has less power to discourage or frustrate you. You'll even see some of the unfair things that happen to you become the building blocks to a life you could not experience without disappointment. This worldview makes God's gospel counterintuitive to our native thinking.

Time to Reflect

1. Does your life reflect a "what's in it for me" attitude, or do you focus on "how can I serve others"? The self-centered life will think primarily on unfairness, while the other-centered life trusts in a God who judges justly.
2. What do your responses to disappointments reveal about your heart? Perhaps considering the last unfair thing that has happened to you will help with this reflection. Where do you need to change?

Ask the Lord to help you examine your heart and practice Christlike responses when life feels unfair.

Let's live boldly, trusting God's wisdom and goodness, even in a broken world.

Day 3

Parents Aren't Perfect

Today's topic might hit close to home: learning to accept that your parents aren't perfect. It's easy to agree that nobody's perfect—until someone's imperfections directly affect you. One of the most painful lessons I had to learn as a young adult was to accept my parents' shortcomings. Our children are no different; they live with imperfect parents, which is not a justification but a fact of reality.

> God, I thank you that I am not like other men.
>
> (Luke 18:11)

When Expectations Collide with Reality

What I wanted from my parents didn't match who they were as fallen individuals. I didn't understand that my desire for them to change couldn't override the reality of their unique struggles, personal baggage, and shaping influences, which had nothing to do with me. They had no mentors or guidance and, like me, were caught in the confusion of life without Christ. Ironically, I expected them to be good people while I was blind to my own selfishness and sin.

Looking back, I realize I should have pitied them instead of responding with anger. But self-absorbed, entitled, and demanding people (like I was) rarely show compassion to others who are more like them than unlike them. It wasn't until my early twenties that I stopped to consider why I had been so angry with them. Here are four reasons that stand out.

1. **LIFE WAS OVERWHELMING:** As a youth, life was moving too fast for me to process. I couldn't handle everything happening around me. Instead of slowing down and seeking help, I lashed out.

2. **MY PARENTS WERE FALLEN PEOPLE:** Like all of us, my parents were faithful to their Adamic natures. They weren't Christians at the time, and their behavior was consistent with who they were. I expected more from them than they could give. Even if they were believers, they would continue to be imperfect.

3. **MY MIND WAS CHAOTIC:** The noise inside my head was deafening. My thoughts were like a busy intersection where too much was happening at once, leaving no space for clarity or grace. Blind to your own blindness is the worst kind of blindness.

4. **I WANTED ESCAPE, NOT CHANGE:** My goal was to leave home rather than seek personal growth that the challenges held out for me. I thought physical distance would solve my problems, but it didn't. You carry who you are wherever you are. The goal is to realize that it's less about them and more about you.

A Friend's Advice

A friend once told me, "Your attitude will affect your altitude. You can soar with the eagles or cluck with the chickens." While it sounded like something from a bumper sticker, he was right. Blaming others for my struggles was a recipe for bitterness. I had to stop playing the victim card and take responsibility for what depended upon me.

Time to Reflect

If you're frustrated with your parents, take a step back and ask yourself these questions:

1.   Are you asking your parents to be something you refuse to be? Are you holding them to a higher standard than you hold yourself?
2.   How is your example presenting Christ to your parents? Are you showing them the same grace, patience, and humility that Christ has shown you?

Accepting that your parents are imperfect doesn't mean excusing sin, but it does mean responding with compassion and humility. Instead of demanding change from them, focus on how you can reflect Christ to them. As you grow in grace, you might be surprised at how God works through your example.

Let's live boldly, trusting God to transform our hearts and our relationships.

Day 4

Forget About Self-Esteem

Let's confront a popular but harmful idea: self-esteem. Our culture teaches that we need to esteem and think highly of ourselves. While it's true that you should see yourself as a unique individual created in God's image—what we call the Imago Dei, self-esteem, as the world defines it—putting yourself first—is a trap that elevates you while diminishes others. This way of thinking leads to internal frustration, external pride, and ongoing disappointment.

> "Teacher, which is the great commandment in the Law?" And he said to him, "You shall love the Lord your God with all your heart and with all your soul and with all your mind. This is the great and first commandment. And a second is like it: You shall love your neighbor as yourself. On these two commandments depend all the Law and the Prophets."
>
> (Matthew 22:36-40).

What the Bible Teaches

Biblical love for yourself is grounded in humility and wisdom—never devaluing the Imago Dei and determined to steer away from self-focus. The two great commandments in Matthew 22:36-40 remind us to love God and love others as we love ourselves. The assumption is we already love ourselves, releasing us to focus on loving God and others well. Turning inward, especially during hard times, will only increase despair (Philippians 2:3-4). Biblical success focuses on serving God and benefiting others, not elevating yourself above God and others.

A Personal Story

Perhaps you've been tempted toward self-focus because you don't know any other way. That was true for me. My parents were inadequate leaders who violated and abandoned me, leaving me to figure out life on my own. I learned to be self-reliant, which seemed like a solution, but it kept me locked in a self-focused mindset. I became the proverbial dog thrown into a pond, told to sink or swim. I swam, but I did so in my strength, which only deepened my despair—the only outcome for the self-reliant soul.

It wasn't until I was 25 that I learned my best life wasn't found in myself but in someone else—Jesus Christ. That was the day God regenerated me, and I surrendered my life to Him. I soon stopped complaining about my circumstances, took responsibility for my choices, and trusted Him to change me. Submitting to Christ made all the difference.

The True Antidote to Self-Focus

If you want to find true value, stop trying to lift yourself up and respond to God by giving your life to Christ. He can do for you what you cannot do for yourself. Your worth and purpose aren't found in other people's opinions or your achievements but in the One who created you.

Instead of trying to feel better about yourself by looking inward or demanding validation from others, focus on serving God and loving those around you. As you pour out your life for Christ, you will find joy, purpose, and the fulfillment you've been longing for. Seeking satisfaction through any other means will only lead to despair.

Time to Reflect

1. How has the self-esteem worldview influenced the way you think about yourself? Has it encouraged self-focus or reliance on God?
2. How do you think finding your identity in Christ will change your desires, needs, and beliefs about yourself?

Take time today to examine where you're looking for your worth. Surrender your self-focused thoughts to Christ, and let Him show you how to live a life of service, humility, and joy. True freedom and fulfillment come when you stop striving to lift yourself up and rest in the love of your Savior. Let's live boldly, trusting God to transform your understanding of who you are in Him.

Day 5

Wait Until You Get a Boss

One of life's great lessons is learning to respond well when you don't get what you want—a challenge for 100 out of every 100 people. Coincidentally, if you think that not getting what you want is just something kids deal with, think again. Life is full of unmet expectations, and how you respond to those expectations now will shape your ability to handle the challenges ahead. The good news? Learning to respond humbly to disappointment is a key to living well in God's world.

> Blessed is the man who remains steadfast under trial, for when he has stood the test he will receive the crown of life, which God has promised to those who love him.
>
> (James 1:12)

Difficult People Are Everywhere

Have you ever felt like your parents, teachers, or other authority figures were too tough on you? Maybe you've thought, "They don't understand me," or "They don't give me what I deserve." The truth is, everyone has difficult people in their lives—no exceptions. And here's the reality: there will always be someone in your life who disappoints you and doesn't meet your expectations.

For example, someday, you'll have a boss. Every job comes with one; no matter your profession, there will always be an authority over you. Even if you're self-employed, your customers will be—somewhat—authorities. And when that day comes, guess what? Your boss won't be perfect either. If you get married, you'll quickly realize you've married another imperfect person. If you don't learn now how to live with or respond well to disappointing people, your future troubles will multiply.

The Root of the Problem

I used to think most of my problems came from my parents. Then I got a job and realized my frustrations at work were eerily similar to the ones I had at home. The issue wasn't my parents or my boss—it was me. Thankfully, God stepped into my life and gave me another perspective. When I was born again (John 3:7), He helped me see that I had been living with a victim mentality. I had been blaming others for my struggles instead of taking responsibility for my reactions and trusting Him to guide me.

If you think your parents are hard, and your first reaction is sinful anger or frustration toward them, brace yourself. Life will be hard for you until you address the real problem: your own heart. Your parents, your boss, or anyone else aren't your biggest issue or barrier to a successful life. You are. But there is hope: the sooner you apply gospel truths to your life, the better it will be.

Gospel Solutions for Life's Disappointments

Instead of blaming others, ask God to reorient your thinking and help you respond to disappointment with humility. Jesus modeled this for us. Though He was treated unfairly, He entrusted Himself to God (1 Peter 2:23). His example shows us how to rise above frustration and trust God's plan.

Time to Reflect

1. How do you typically respond when others disappoint you? Your reactions to unmet desires reveal your level of maturity. Are you growing in humility, or are you stuck in anger, grumbling, and frustration?

2. What do your responses to frustrations reveal about your relationship with God? Do they point to trust and dependence on Him or self-centered thinking?

Take time today to consider how you typically respond to disappointment. Ask the Lord to show you areas where you need to grow, and trust Him to help you move forward. Life will always have its challenges, but with Christ at the center, you can navigate them with grace and maturity.

Let's live boldly, choosing humility and trust in the One who never disappoints.

Day 6

Life Is Mundane; Get Used to It

I want to share with you something many people overlook: the beauty of a mundane life. Your grandparents might have called it real life—the everyday, ordinary moments of living in an imperfect world. While the culture chases the next big thing, the spiritual person recognizes that even the most mundane moments are opportunities to glorify God. Hidden in the ordinary are the blessings that only a spiritual mind can see.

> For my thoughts are not your thoughts, neither are your ways my ways, declares the LORD. For as the heavens are higher than the earth, so are my ways higher than your ways and my thoughts than your thoughts.
>
> (Isaiah 55:8-9)

The Blessings in Mundanity

Could your present boring challenges be the very opportunities you need to grow and mature? The Lord often uses trials to teach us character qualities that will shape the course of our lives (2 Corinthians 1:8-9). God's lessons are hard, but they are designed to transform you into a better person, someone who reflects His image more clearly.

It's easy to misunderstand what God is doing in our lives, especially when it doesn't match our desires, wishes, or expectations. Human wisdom says the mundane is boring, even pointless. But God's wisdom says the mundane is the primary place where transformation happens. Recognizing these moments as opportunities takes spiritual maturity, insight, and actionable steps.

Even Christ's Life Seemed Mundane

Think about Jesus. To many, He seemed like just another man from Nazareth. Even His adoring disciples struggled to understand His higher purpose, especially when He talked about dying on a cross (Mark 8:31-33). But Jesus used what seemed ordinary to accomplish extraordinary things. He turned the world upside down through humble, everyday acts of obedience.

In the same way, don't underestimate your life. A dead-end job, a difficult class, or a quiet season at home are not obstacles to God's plan. They are the very places where He is working in you and through you.

Find Christ in the Mundane

Your mission is to locate Christ in your circumstances. Where is Jesus working in the mundane moments of your life today? Don't rush through the mundane, trying to escape. Instead, ask, "What is God doing here?" and "How can I glorify Him in the ordinary routines of my life?"

The details of your life—big or small—are not random or meaningless. God is in the details. When you seek Him in everyday circumstances, you'll discover the contentment and purpose that only He can give. And as you grow in this mindset, your life will have a redemptive impact on those around you.

Time to Reflect

1. What does it mean to see Christ in your circumstances—seeing Him as the center of your story, trusting that He is working even in the ordinary, and asking how you can honor Him in the here and now?

2. How will finding Christ in your problems change your problems? How will it shift your perspective, helping you see your challenges as opportunities for growth and transformation? Rather than obstacles, your problems become platforms for God's glory and your good.

Take time today to think about the mundane moments in your life. Ask God to give you spiritual eyes to see His purposes in them. When you embrace the ordinary as an opportunity to grow and glorify Him, you will experience contentment and joy that only the Lord can provide.

Let's live boldly, trusting God in the details of every moment.

Day 7

Your Mistakes Are Yours

Today's lesson is tough but essential: when you mess up, it's no one's fault but your own. It's natural to want to blame others for our mistakes. Perhaps others are part of our mistakes or have influenced them. However, we cannot ignore our responsibility. We must not permit people's problems to manage us. Adults struggle with owning their mistakes, so you're not alone. But if your first instinct is to point fingers when things go wrong, it's time to pause, recalibrate that mindset, and take responsibility. Owning your mistakes is a key step toward maturity and spiritual growth.

For each will have to bear his own load.

(Galatians 6:5)

Anger and Its Root Cause

When things don't go your way, how do you react? Complaining, whining, or grumbling might seem harmless, but they are subtle forms of anger. James 4:1-3 offers insight into this matter, asking, "What causes quarrels and fights among you?" The answer lies within you. James explains that sinful anger comes from unmet passions, desires, and coveting—internal and warring heart idols that reveal what you value most.

Instead of looking outward for someone to blame, ask yourself what your anger reveals about you. Sinful anger often surfaces when you don't get what you want. Have you considered that not getting all you want might be the very thing God is using to shape you into the person He wants you to be?

Learning from Jesus' Example

Even Jesus faced an "I'm not getting what I want" moment in the Garden of Gethsemane. As He prepared for the cross, He prayed, "Father, if you are willing, remove this cup from me. Nevertheless, not my will, but yours, be done" (Luke 22:42). I'm not suggesting that Jesus made a mistake here or any mistakes at all. However, Jesus didn't want to endure the pain of the cross, but He submitted His desires to His Father's will.

His example is your best option when you're struggling with anger or disappointment. You may not always get what you want, but you can choose to submit your life to God. When you do, your anger and angst will subside, and you'll gain clarity on how to respond to life's challenges.

Taking Responsibility

Owning your mistakes and submitting to God's will are not easy steps, but they are necessary for growth. Blaming others keeps you stuck in an endless rut, while taking responsibility moves you forward. Instead of asking, "Who's at fault?" ask, "What does this problem reveal about me?" and "How can I grow from this?" God will use sin sinlessly. Meaning that the sinful things that happen, whether your fault or others, can have redemptive and restorative purposes.

Time to Reflect

1. What does your anger reveal about you? Is it pointing to a specific desire or expectation that you've placed above God's will?
2. Will you take the time to write out a specific and practical plan for change? Consider sharing it with a trusted mentor who can encourage and guide you.

Take time today to examine your heart. Pray for God to show you areas where you need to grow, and trust Him to help you submit your life to His good and perfect plan.

Let's live boldly, owning our mistakes and trusting God to work out all things for His glory and our good.

Day 8

Your Parents Weren't Always Boring

Your parents weren't always boring. Believe it or not, they had lives, interests, and a lot more freedom before you came along. Here's the truth: your parents' lives changed dramatically the moment you entered the picture. It's not that you're a problem; I'm not saying that at all, but raising a child comes with enormous responsibility. Paying bills, doing laundry, and keeping up with your needs leave little time for the fun or spontaneity they had prior to having children. Their sacrifices are often invisible, but they are made out of love for you and the belief that their life is worth more than their former freedoms. Parenting is a picture of the gospel: giving up your freedom for the good of others.

> See to it that no one fails to obtain the grace of God; that no "root of bitterness" springs up and causes trouble, and by it many become defiled.
> (Hebrews 12:15)

A Call to Honor Your Parents

Before you move out to start your life, take a moment to think about what your parents have done for you. May I frame it this way: Do you have high expectations for how others should treat you while neglecting to honor the sacrifices your parents have made? One way to show gratitude is by pitching in to help with household responsibilities. Small acts of service can go a long way in showing them respect and appreciation.

What If Your Parents Haven't Been Great?

Maybe your experience is different. Perhaps your parents haven't sacrificed for you or have failed in real ways. Maybe you've felt more like a burden to them than a blessing. If that's the case, I'm sorry for your experience. It's painful when parents fail to fulfill their God-given roles. But even if your parents haven't led well, you can choose a different path—not by reacting sinfully to them but by responding redemptively to God.

What if you became the responsible one in your family? Instead of letting their failures define you, you can rise above and become the grown-up in the room. Parental irresponsibility doesn't have to be your destiny. You can break the cycle and create a new legacy for your future family.

Don't Carry the Chip

For years, I carried a chip on my shoulder because I felt cheated by life, especially by my parents. My bitterness grew into resentment and unforgiveness, poisoning my heart and clouding my judgment. Eventually, I realized I was no better than my parents. I complained about their failures without addressing my own. The Bible word for this is hypocrisy. One day, your parents will no longer be here. When that day comes, the choices you make will be entirely your own. Blaming them won't be an option then. It would prove wise to respond differently today.

Time to Reflect

1. If you have good parents, how are you showing them gratitude? Are you practicing honor by serving and appreciating them?
2. If your parents haven't been great, how are you working to make your life and your family history different? What steps can you take to change the narrative in your home, setting up a restorative pattern for your future family?

Take time today to reflect on your relationship with your parents. Whether they've been faithful or fallen short, you have the opportunity to honor them and grow into the person God has called you to be.

Let's live boldly, choosing gratitude, forgiveness, and responsibility as we build lives that glorify God.

Day 9

Life Has Losers; Don't Be One

Today's topic may sound harsh, but it's an essential truth to embrace: life has winners and losers. I know that you know this, but I want to make it personal to you during this season of practical reflection. Participation trophies and grade inflation may soften the blow during childhood, but adulthood operates by a different set of rules. The self-esteem movement works hard to keep kids' egos inflated, but life in a fallen world works harder, deflating our egos, making it imperative we know how to live well when fallenness falls on us.

> Whatever you do, work heartily, as for the Lord and not for men, knowing that from the Lord you will receive the inheritance as your reward. You are serving the Lord Christ.
>
> (Colossians 3:23-24)

Childhood Perks Don't Last

When in school or playing sports as a kid, you might get extra chances to succeed. Retaking a failed test or receiving a trophy for simply showing up for the game can make life seem more forgiving—and even equitable. But in the adult world, things work differently. Adult mistakes have negative consequences, and sometimes, those consequences stick with you for a long time. Life can leave a mark.

That doesn't mean failure is hopeless. You can mess up and still recover, but the cost of failure often increases as you grow older. A boo-boo as a kid is a calamity for adults. This harsh truth is why preparing for adulthood now is so critical. The habits you're building today will shape how you handle the challenges of tomorrow.

Maturity Starts Now

Adulthood doesn't automatically make you mature. Maturity isn't about age; it's about the condition of your heart. Many adults act like kids, and a plethora of kids behave adult-like. The good news is that you don't have to wait until you're older to start maturing. These early adult years are like a laboratory where you can experiment with life: try, fail, adjust, and try again.

To fail is not a problem unless you let your failures define and paralyze you. Every successful person became that way by moving down a path strewn with failures. The goal is to flip negative episodes in your life into sporadic successes that eventually become consistent patterns. When you start developing habits of responsibility, discipline, and perseverance, you'll be ready to handle adulthood when it comes—and it will come whether you're ready or not.

Life doesn't wait for you to feel prepared. If you enter adulthood without the tools to navigate it, you will not do well. The way to prepare is to start now. Take stock of your life and your habits. Are you building a foundation for maturity, or are you relying on the safety nets of childhood to carry you?

Time to Reflect

1. What does it mean to prepare for adulthood? Think about the habits and character traits you'll need to thrive in the adult world. Are you practicing responsibility, humility, and perseverance today?
2. Who's preparing you for adulthood? Are you seeking guidance from parents, mentors, or trusted adults? If not, who can you ask to walk with you as you navigate this season? What are your plans for growth and maturity?

Take some time to pray and ask God to help you see where you need to grow. Surround yourself with people who will challenge and encourage you to mature in Christ. Remember, adulthood isn't something to fear—it's an opportunity to glorify God with your life.

Let's live boldly, preparing today for the challenges of tomorrow.

Day 10

You Don't Get Time Off

The rest of your life does not come with summers off. In school, you get days off—snow days, holiday breaks, and long summer vacations. Many kids complain the summers need to be longer and school is too hard. But once they step into adulthood, the rhythm changes. There are no built-in summers off, and life becomes a long, steady mundane journey—one that ends only when you drop dead and step into eternity. This perspective might not sound very encouraging, but it's actually an opportunity to rethink your mindset about work, rest, and the purpose of your life.

> Whatever your hand finds to do, do it with your might, for there is no work or thought or knowledge or wisdom in Sheol, to which you are going.
> (Ecclesiastes 9:10)

The Trap of Weekend Chasing

If you complain about school being too long, too hard, or too boring, you might be tempted to carry that same bad attitude into adulthood. Habits are patterns, and bad habits are like walking around with concrete shoes. Adults who dread their work often find themselves pining for the next weekend, living for two short days of unsatisfying rest while the remainder of their week feels like a slog. This cyclic pattern is as unfulfilling as it sounds, debilitating to their growth and complicating for their relationships.

Resting is good and proper, but it should always be something other than the highlight of your week. Instead, think about how you can approach work with purpose and joy, knowing that God has called you to live for His glory. Don't let school or a transitional job put you into the trap of living for the weekend. Find rest in your work, which might mean spending time at your school or mundane career on activities that transform lives—yours and others?

Your Value in God's Kingdom

Don't think Christianity is something you graduate into when you become an adult. God's call on your life begins now. You are just as valuable in His kingdom as any adult with a full-time job (1 Timothy 4:12).

What is your purpose? How has God gifted you? How can you use those gifts today to serve Him and others? Life with God isn't something you put off until you're older; it's a journey that begins now. Align your heart with God's plans, not the cultural expectations for young people.

Using Your Time Wisely

Even your breaks, like summer vacation, should be opportunities to prepare for the future. How can you use those times to grow, learn, and serve? Consider asking trusted adults in your life for advice about how to integrate work and rest in a way that glorifies God.

Time to Reflect

1. Are you fun-centered or work-centered? When you have free time, do you focus more on serving yourself or others?
2. What is one specific and practical way you can change your perspective on work and fun? For example, could you set aside time each week to serve in your church, volunteer, or develop a skill that benefits others?

Take time today to evaluate your priorities. Pray and ask God to help you align your heart with His purpose for your life. A fulfilling life isn't found in chasing fun or escaping work; it's found in working hard for the Lord and finding joy in serving others.

Let's live boldly, seeing each day as an opportunity to glorify God, no matter the task.

Day 11

Social Media Is Not Real Life

Let's explore a topic that affects us all: the shaping influences in our lives—those things external to us that impact how we love God and others as we love ourselves. Specifically, how social media and other technologies shape the way we think, feel, and live.

> Do not be deceived: "Bad company ruins good morals."
>
> (1 Corinthians 15:33)

What Influences You?

The two most powerful forces shaping your life are what you allow into your mind and the people you surround yourself with. I'm speaking of the things you permit to feed and mold your brain. Take time to reflect. Who influences your desires, decisions, and destiny? My question is crucial because your answers reveal a lot about who you are and are becoming. Everyone is brainwashed in the sense that we allow things to wash over our minds, leaving residuals that mature into influences that provide interpretive filters through which we see and respond to life.

For example, you are a reflection of the media you consume and the company you keep. As a Christian, your ultimate goals are to love God and others as you love yourself. To do that well, you need influences that point you toward those goals. If the media you consume or the friends you associate with pull you away from the two greatest commandments, it's time to make a change.

The Battle for Your Mind

Media includes everything from TV shows, movies, and social platforms to books, music, and websites. While these tools can be used for good, they also have the power to shape your mind in unwholesome ways. The enemy uses worldly influences to capture your thoughts and distract you from Christ (2 Corinthians 10:3-6).

But you can flip the script. Even if negativity and harmful influences have been a part of your story so far, God can redeem your mind and heart. Genesis 50:20 reminds us that God can take what was meant for harm and use it for good. Philippians 4:8 encourages us to focus on what is true, honorable, and pure.

A Personal Choice

After I became a Christian, I made a deliberate choice to let the Bible be my primary influence. I jokingly call it "Bible brainwashing," but it's true—I immersed myself in God's Word and surrounded myself with Christian friends who were passionate about Jesus. While I couldn't avoid the world's influence entirely, I could choose what I allowed to shape my mind and heart primarily.

You're not just floating aimlessly through life as though you are disconnected from others or their habits. Every day, you're being influenced by someone or something, and you're influencing others in return. You do have control over what those influences will be. The first step toward spiritual maturity is deciding what captivates your mind. Everybody will serve somebody, but we're not hapless victims with no power or agency. We must choose wisely regarding those people, places, and things that will take up space in our minds.

Time to Reflect

1. To what degree do God's Word and His community influence your life? Are you immersing yourself in Scripture and surrounding yourself with people who encourage you to grow in Christ?
2. How do you make the Bible practically relevant to your life? Be specific. For example, do you start your day by reading and reflecting on Scripture? Do you apply what you learn to your relationships, choices, and priorities?

Take time to evaluate your media and relationships. Ask yourself if they are helping you love God and others more deeply. If not, pray for courage to make changes.

Let's live boldly, choosing influences that point us to Christ and help us grow in Him.

Day 12

Coolness Is Not the Path to Success

L et's tackle a common cultural myth: the idea that being "cool" is the way to succeed. The truth is that chasing coolness is rarely fruitful. Instead, it often leads to dysfunctional relationships and a self-focused, enslaving way of life that demands that others notice, admire, and desire to be you. Perhaps it would serve all of us if we redefine what it means to be "cool" from a biblical perspective.

> He was despised and rejected by men, a man of sorrows and acquainted with grief; and as one from whom men hide their faces he was despised, and we esteemed him not.
>
> (Isaiah 53:3)

Biblical "Coolness" Is Countercultural

The world's definition of coolness revolves around self-promotion and comparison. You measure yourself against others, striving to meet shifting standards of popularity, style, or status. The insecure soul that craves the approval of others will scan the cultural landscape for the most popular fads and acclimate and adorn their themselves accordingly, only to pivot when the cultural winds of change blow again. Biblical coolness looks nothing like the culture's zeitgeist.

Consider Isaiah 53:1-7, where Christ is described as "unesteemed," "unlovely," "unappealing," and "unacceptable." These words are the opposite of cool, yet they perfectly describe Jesus. He wasn't focused on fitting in or impressing others. Oh, He drew passionate followers. Why? Because true greatness isn't about conforming; it's about living in alignment with God and His purposes.

Jesus: The Ultimate Outlier

Imagine Jesus as a young adult. He likely was not overly concerned with impressing others. His focus was on His mission and honoring His Father. His toga might not have been the trendiest, and His priorities didn't match the culture's. He stood out because eternal values, not fleeting popularity, drove His life. Ironically, something was appealing about Jesus. He was not a rebel without a cause, and He did not rebel just to be different.

He was dialed in on His Father's purpose, which put Him out-of-alignment with the world, making Himself God's choice as our leader (1 Corinthians 1:18-25). The life of Christ underscores a powerful truth: success in God's kingdom isn't about strength, popularity, or cultural approval. It's about humility, obedience, and faithfulness.

The Competing Paths: Godly or Cool?

Being godly and cool often pull in opposite directions if your primary concern is cultural assumptions. To pursue godliness, you'll likely have to let go of worldly definitions of success. Jesus said, "I am the way, the truth, and the life" (John 14:6), reminding us that His path is right—even when it feels countercultural.

Time to Reflect

1. Whose opinion matters most: God's or the culture's? Your answer reveals what influences you the most. Why did you answer the way you did? If you find yourself prioritizing culture, reflect on how God's eternal truth offers something far better than fleeting trends.

2. What keeps you from fully identifying as a Christian? Is it fear of standing out, rejection, or losing popularity? Be honest about your struggles, and ask God to help you trust Him more deeply.

Take time to evaluate your priorities. Are you chasing approval, or are you pursuing a life that honors Christ? Remember, the world's version of cool is temporary, but following Jesus leads to eternal purpose and joy.

Let's live boldly, choosing the path of godliness over fleeting popularity.

Day 13

Life Is Hard and Doesn't Apologize

Today's truth may not be easy to hear, but it's crucial to understand: life is hard and doesn't apologize. Fallenness is no respecter of persons, not even caring if you are a Christian. Everyone faces struggles, but what sets people apart is how they respond to their life challenges, which begs the question. Will you choose to complain and remain stuck in your trouble, or will you flip the script and become a difference-maker?

> For the righteous falls seven times and rises again,
> but the wicked stumble in times of calamity.
> (Proverbs 24:16)

The Choice Is Yours

Life's difficulties aren't about fairness or exceptions; they're about what you choose to do with what comes your way. The Bible teaches that your response to trials can glorify God and transform you into the person He created you to be. Even when life seems unfair, you have the opportunity to rise above it and put God's name on display.

This mindset shift is powerful and appears to be a rare jewel in this generation of disgruntled souls. Your story is defined not by the circumstances themselves but by your response to them, making your impulses and reactions the materials that will bring shape to your life.

My Story of Blame and Transformation

As a teenager, I didn't understand this truth. By age 15, I was angry, reckless, and sitting in jail for the bad decisions I had made. I didn't take responsibility for my actions. Instead, I blamed others, convinced that my problems were someone else's fault. Sure, there were people in my life who genuinely hurt me. But when you mix disappointment with a legitimate complaint, you're standing at the edge of victimhood. I took that next step into self-pity, and it was a trap that I could not see until I was ensnared by it.

It wasn't until Christ got hold of my life that I realized I didn't have to live this way. The bad things that happened to me didn't have to define me negatively. I could allow Christ to transform me from the inside out, giving me a new identity and purpose. This new life did not erase my past mistakes but it did reinterpret them through a redemptive filter that gave me a passion and purpose to serve others. God does use sin sinlessly.

Transcend Your Troubles

The best decision you can make is to follow Jesus. If you fall, get back up and keep following Jesus. Your most transformative and memorable lessons will come through your failures. Life's hardships don't have to control you when you belong to Him. As part of God's family, you have the strength to transcend your troubles and turn them into opportunities for growth and witness. It's called flipping the narrative by taking what was meant for evil and using it for good (Genesis 50:20).

You will submit to someone or something—whether it's your circumstances, the opinions of others, or the cravings of your heart. Why not submit to Christ? He offers hope, healing, and the power to flip your negative narrative into a story of redemption and purpose.

Time to Reflect

1. How do you usually respond to disappointments? What is your typical reaction to life's challenges? Are you quick to blame, complain, or give up? Or, are you quick to see God's purpose in the problems?
2. What is one thing you can do to flip one of your negative narratives? How can you reframe it as an opportunity to grow, serve others, or glorify God?

Take time today to ask God for wisdom and courage to respond to life's difficulties in a way that honors Him. You can't control what life throws at you, but you can choose how to respond, which will make all the difference.

Let's live boldly, choosing to transcend life's hardships by relying on Christ's transformative power.

Day 14

Where to Go from Here?

L et's reflect on God's grace and its power to guide you through life's challenges. Here is how I want to frame God's grace for this devotion: No matter what you're facing, God's grace is sufficient, offering answers to your questions and untangling the messiest problems. The question then becomes: Where will you go from here— wherever you may be at this juncture in your journey with the Lord?

> Trust in the LORD with all your heart, and do not lean on your own understanding. In all your ways acknowledge him, and he will make straight your paths.
>
> (Proverbs 3:5-6)

Trust God's Grace

Despair, discouragement, or depression over your disappointments are not the solutions to what is happening in your life. God calls you to trust Him, even when the obstacles seem overwhelming. As you think about the next steps, consider these six tips to help you apply God's transforming grace.

Six Tips for Moving Forward

1. **BREAK FREE FROM UNHELPFUL INFLUENCES:** Genetic, familial, or cultural influences don't control your life. Even your bad choices do not exert perpetual power over your life. You can break free from what binds you and build a satisfying life rooted in God's truth. Ask yourself: What is the primary control shaping my life?

2. **START WITH THE GOSPEL:** Real and lasting change begins with the gospel—the person and work of Christ in your life. When the gospel is your starting point, it will also be your pathway and destination. Is your life grounded in the good news of Jesus Christ?

3. **EXAMINE YOUR WORSHIP:** Everyone, everywhere worships something; God wired us to worship. Thus, we ask, "Who or what are we worshiping?" Take time to evaluate the primary object of your worship. Are you bowing to God or something less worthy?

4. **FOCUS ON THE HEART, NOT JUST BEHAVIOR:** All change begins in the heart. There is wisdom in amputating things from your life (Matthew 5:29), but the source of our attitudes and thoughts that lead to actions is in our hearts (Luke 6:45). Ask yourself: What heart change can you make to alter your behaviors?

5. **LET TRANSFORMATION BE ABOUT GOD:** A lack of growth isn't just about your parents, your circumstances, or even yourself—it's about God, the Author and Finisher of your faith. Let Him be the starting point for all you do. What does your attitude toward your parents (or others in authority) reveal about your relationship with God? If you are angry at someone, you must recognize that God is permitting these circumstances.

6. **SALVATION IS JUST THE BEGINNING:** Salvation isn't the finish line but the beginning of a lifelong journey to glorify God. After regeneration, you begin a life of progressive, incremental sanctification. How have you been changing since the day God saved you? What fruit is evident in your life?

Time to Reflect

Choose one of these six tips for reflection. Write out a specific plan to apply it to your life. For example:

1. If you choose to focus on the gospel, consider spending time each day meditating on a key verse, such as Romans 1:16 or John 3:16.
2. If you choose to examine your worship, list the things that compete for your attention and ask God to help you re-center your heart on Him.

Share what the Lord is teaching you with a trusted mentor or friend. Let them encourage and hold you accountable as you grow.

Let's live boldly, embracing God's grace and allowing it to transform our lives for His glory.

Day 15

While You're Waiting, Do These

Do you ever sense your life as a young adult is in a holding pattern—a time when you're just waiting for life to begin? If so, you're not alone. Some people act as though these early years are like an extended time out. It is a mindset that can lead to wasting valuable time. While you're waiting to get your shot, here are eight things you can do to steward your time well and glorify God today. The key to remember is what you do today forms the foundation upon which your entire adult life will stand. If you procrastinate, as though life does not begin until later, you may develop the debilitating habit of procrastination.

> Look carefully then how you walk, not as unwise but as wise, making the best use of the time, because the days are evil.
>
> (Ephesians 5:15-16)

Eight Things to Do While You Wait

1. **WORSHIP:** God is our satisfaction. Life's busyness might compete for your attention and fill your calendar, but it's essential to fight for time with God. Make Him your priority, even with an overwhelming schedule.
2. **HOPE:** God's plans often seem slow, though His

delays are intentional. He uses waiting to teach gratitude, patience, perseverance, and other character traits you will need all your life. Keep your hope rooted in God's goodness, trusting that He is working in your life today.

3. **REST:** Avoid the temptation to force life to happen on your terms. Resting while waiting is a gift from God. Instead of forcing yourself on the game, let the game come to you while trusting God's plan to unfold at the right time.

4. **TRUST:** Life's difficulties aren't barriers to life— they're opportunities to put Christ on display. Like resistance training, you become stronger with each rep. Embrace adversity as a chance to grow in faith and show others the power of trusting God.

5. **IMITATE:** There are always people around you who are unseen and unheard. These souls feel the pinch of loneliness daily. Look beyond yourself and seek out those who are struggling. Be a living testimony of the love of Christ by encouraging and caring for them. Who will you be Jesus to today?

6. **REPENT:** Repentance is a gift from God. For too many believers, it's the rustiest tool in their toolshed. It allows you to turn from sin and align your life with the Lord's will. Like a superhero with a secret weapon, you can change your life by actively and practically repenting.

7. **PRAY:** Ask God for what you need, and trust His response, especially if He does not give you what you want or delays His response. Your job isn't to worry about whether He'll give you what you want; it's to ask in faith and prepare your heart for His answer.

8. **GRATITUDE:** Your attitude when you don't get what you ask for reveals the strength of your faith. Cultivate gratitude in all circumstances—big and

small. A thankful heart is a mature heart. A "No" from the Lord means He has something better in mind.

Time to Reflect

Choose one tip from the list to focus on. For example:

1. If you choose gratitude, start a daily gratitude journal. Write down three things you're thankful for each day, and reflect on how they reveal God's goodness to you.
2. If you choose prayer, set aside a specific time daily to pray about what's on your heart and ask God to align your desires with His will.

Write a specific plan to implement your chosen tip. Share it with a trusted mentor who can encourage and hold you accountable. Waiting doesn't have to feel like wasted time. Use this season to grow, serve, and draw closer to God. You don't have to wait for the future to glorify Him—start today.

Let's live boldly, making the most of the present as we wait with faith and purpose.

Day 16

Your Local Church

One of the most essential places for your spiritual growth is the local church. Outside of your home, the local church is the dearest place on earth for a believer because it's where God's people gather to worship, grow, and serve together. The church is not a building but a body of believers, whether it's two gathered for fellowship or two thousand in an auditorium.

> Now you are the body of Christ and individually members of it.
>
> (1 Corinthians 12:27)

The Bible's timeline for your sanctification starts at regeneration (new birth) and ends at glorification (a new body). Your local church plays a vital role in this process. To experience daily, ongoing change, you must be actively engaged in the life of your church. Here are three key factors to help you mature through this means of grace:

1. **AFFECTION:** Do you love your local assembly? A high view of the church is essential for transformation. Your local church is a visible manifestation of Christ's body, and your affection for it is directly tied to your spiritual soundness. Do you value and prioritize your church, or is it just another part of your schedule?

2. **TRAINING:** Does your church provide the resources and training you need for sanctification? This might include preaching, small group studies, mentoring contexts, or service projects. The purpose of these is to help you grow in your relationship with Christ. Are you taking advantage of the training your church offers? If not, what's holding you back?

3. **COMMUNITY:** Christianity isn't a spectator sport. You can't grow in isolation. The church is a community where believers actively encourage and sharpen one another (Hebrews 10:24-25). Serving others not only helps them grow but matures you in the process. Are you an active participant in your church, or merely attending without engaging?

Sustained Change Takes Time

Transformation happens in time. It's a lifelong process of work and dependence on God's grace. Consistent growth requires being part of a biblical community. If your current church isn't helping, you have two options: Become a catalyst for positive change by serving and encouraging others, or find a church that fosters discipleship.

Before leaving—if you must, seek advice from trusted mentors to ensure you're making the right decision.

Avoid Isolation

Don't be a silo Christian who detaches from the life of the church. Relationships in real-world contexts are essential for growth. Cyber-communities can supplement your faith, but they can't replace the accountability, fellowship, and encouragement found in face-to-face relationships within the body-to-body ministries of a local church.

Time to Reflect

1. Is your church the right disciple-making context for you? How do you know? If you're considering leaving, have you sought wise counsel first?

2. Rather than an exit strategy, how can you help your church become a better disciple-making community? If your church is already strong in discipleship, how can you contribute to making it even better?

Take time to pray for your local church, its leaders, and its members. Ask God how He wants you to serve, grow, and help others within your church family.

Let's live boldly, loving and engaging with the local church as God's chosen means for our growth and His glory.

Day 17

Five Young Adult Traps

Five common traps many young adults face can hinder their growth and keep them from living the life God has for them. The good news is that recognizing these traps is the first step to avoiding them and finding freedom in Christ. I'm sharing them with you in no particular order, though it would serve you to prioritize them according to how they apply to your life.

> This Book of the Law shall not depart from your mouth, but you shall meditate on it day and night, so that you may be careful to do according to all that is written in it. For then you will make your way prosperous, and then you will have good success.
>
> (Joshua 1:8)

Five Traps to Avoid

1. **FEAR:** Fear often manifests as comparing yourself to others. The more insecure you are, the more likely you are to make unwise choices about friends or situations to try to manipulate their acceptance. God calls you to rest in His love; you are fearfully and wonderfully made (Psalm 139:14). You become who God is creating you to be, not what you believe others want you to be.

2. **CONFUSION:** Sometimes, it can seem like God is distant, especially when life feels chaotic, unclear, or static. We old people struggle this way, too. We must remember that God is good, kind, and always attentive. He knows all the details of your life. Trust Him, even when you can't perceive what He's doing (Proverbs 3:5-6).

3. **EXPERIMENTATION:** When you sense emptiness or discontentment, it's tempting to go idol shopping by turning to people, places, or things for worldly pleasure. Experimentation often stems from anger, a low-grade frustration. When life isn't going the way you want, you may look for satisfaction in things that never satisfy. Only Christ can fill the void in your heart (John 4:13-14).

4. **DISCOURAGEMENT:** Young adults are often nitpicked and micro-managed more than they are encouraged. If you're not in an encouraging environment, you might latch onto anyone who gives you the approval you crave. Be careful not to let someone become your functional god. God's approval of you is what truly matters (Galatians 1:10).

5. **DESPAIR:** When fear, confusion, or discouragement pile up, you might succumb to the temptation of giving up on Christianity or giving in to the seductive allurements of the world. Even when surrounded by friends, you can sense a deep loneliness. Know that God sees you, knows you, and offers you hope (Psalm 34:18). You are perfect in Christ, and He loves you more than you can imagine.

Time to Reflect

1. Do any of these traps resonate with you? If so, take time to reflect on where you are and how these struggles might influence your choices. It's not wrong to reach out for help—your church, family, or trusted friends can be a source of grace and support.

2. Who is a competent person in your life who can help you? This individual could be a pastor, a mentor, or a mature friend. Will you reach out to them today?

Don't let fear, confusion, or discouragement keep you trapped. God offers freedom and hope in every situation. Ask Him for wisdom, and surround yourself with people who will encourage and guide you in truth.

Let's live boldly, avoiding these traps and walking confidently in the life God has prepared for us.

Day 18

Who Is a Good Person?

What makes someone good? Before you answer the question about yourself or a friend, I want you to consider this perspective. On the surface, it might seem easy to label someone as good or bad based on their behavior—an external examination, but God calls us to look deeper than outward appearances.

> But the LORD said to Samuel, "Do not look on his appearance or on the height of his stature, because I have rejected him. For the LORD sees not as man sees: man looks on the outward appearance, but the Lord looks on the heart."
>
> (1 Samuel 16:7)

The Danger of Outward Assessments

It's easy to compare yourself with others based on what you can see. Someone who seems to follow all the rules might be labeled good, while someone who struggles outwardly is seen as bad. Outward behavior doesn't always reflect the true state of the heart.

Some young adults learn to perform well in front of others—they know the right words to say and actions to present. This external lifestyle is legalism: behavior driven by appearances rather than a heart transformed by

God. On the other hand, a person who does not fit cultural expectations or seems messy externally might actually have a humble heart—repentant and deeply in love with God.

Biblical Examples of Misjudged People

Consider two women in the New Testament: The widow who gave all she had (Luke 21:1-4) was poor, needy, and insignificant in society's eyes, yet Jesus praised her faith and sacrifice. The sinner woman who anointed Jesus' feet (Luke 7:36-50) was an outcast, despised by others, yet her love and repentance brought her into Jesus' favor. Both of these women would have been dismissed by those focused on outward appearances, but Jesus looked at their hearts and saw faith, love, and humility.

Don't Judge by Appearances

Outward appearances can be deceiving. You might look good on the outside but hide inner turmoil, angst, fears, or idolatries that need God's restorative insight and care. Or you might judge someone for not measuring up outwardly, failing to see how God is working in their life.

Time to Reflect

1. Take time today to examine yourself in two key areas: How do you judge others?
2. Do you assess people primarily based on their appearance or behavior?
3. What does this reveal about your understanding of God's view of the heart? (1 Samuel 16:7)
4. How does God's mercy shape how you treat others?
5. If you've experienced God's forgiveness, how does that influence the way you think about and respond to others?

6. Are you patient, kind, and willing to look past the surface to see what God might be doing in someone?

Ask God to help you see people through His eyes. Pray for humility and wisdom to look past outward appearances and recognize the deeper work He is doing in others—and yourself.

Let's live boldly, focusing on hearts transformed by God rather than outward appearances.

Day 19

Will God Forgive Me?

Today's topic touches on a question many struggle with: "Will God forgive me?" Thinking that the good Lord will not forgive us typically comes from an inward-focused, insecure person who needs a gospel recalibration: Who the Son has set free is free indeed (John 8:36). The gospel liberates us from all of our past sins, no matter how hideous or overwhelming they seem. Jesus has already completed the work of forgiveness—you don't have to live under the weight of guilt any longer.

> There is therefore now no condemnation for those who are in Christ Jesus.
>
> (Romans 8:1)

The Freedom of the Gospel

Some sins seem so massive that they overshadow the truth of the gospel. When your failures seem too great, it's easy to believe that forgiveness is out of reach or that you need something in addition to the gospel. But Jesus' words on the cross, "It is finished" (John 19:30), mean exactly what they say. There is no sin so significant that it falls outside of God's power to forgive.

You don't need to earn God's favor or find another way to pay for your mistakes. The work is done, and the Lord's forgiveness is complete. Will you rest in the completed work of Christ?

The Challenge of Honesty

One of the hardest steps in experiencing forgiveness is being honest about our sins. Admitting where we've gone wrong can feel vulnerable and painful, but this kind of transparency is essential. Without honesty, we risk slipping into self-deception, where we deny our sins or downplay our need for grace.

I've learned through personal experience that hiding sin only leads to deeper guilt and isolation. Recovery begins when we face the truth about ourselves, trusting God's grace to bring restoration.

Four Steps to Freedom

If you're struggling with past sin, here are four steps to help you move forward:

1. **PRAY:** Be honest with God about your sin. He already knows, but telling Him shows your humility and willingness to change.
2. **CONFESS:** Ask God for forgiveness, trusting in His promise to cleanse you from all unrighteousness (1 John 1:9).
3. **RESIST:** Take your thoughts captive, wrestling with the gospel until its power makes you free indeed.
4. **CONFIDE:** Share your struggle with a friend or mentor. A biblical community provides encouragement, support, and accountability as you walk through this process.

Time to Reflect

1. What part of this devotion feels the hardest? Is it admitting your sin, believing in God's forgiveness, taking your thoughts captive, or talking to someone about it? Why is that step difficult for you?
2. Do you have a sin hanging over you like a dark cloud? If so, make a plan to pray, confess, resist, and confide. Don't wait—God's forgiveness is available today.

Take time to reflect on God's mercy. Pray for courage to face your sin honestly and faith to trust in the completeness of Jesus' work on the cross. You don't have to carry guilt any longer—God's forgiveness is real, and His grace is sufficient.

Let's live boldly, living in the freedom and joy that come from a forgiven life.

Day 20

Voice Training

Your conscience that God gave you acts as an internal moral thermostat. It's your inner voice that sounds off when you have done well or poorly. Your conscience can be a powerful tool for aligning your life with God's Word, but it can also become distorted if not biblically trained. The conscience is malleable. Let's talk about how to care for and train your conscience so it reflects God's truth—the ultimate sweet spot is when your inner voice and God's Word are in tune.

> They show that the work of the law is written on their hearts, while their conscience also bears witness, and their conflicting thoughts accuse or even excuse them.
>
> (Romans 2:15)

The Role of Your Conscience

Your conscience reacts to how you respond to life's situations. When you make choices that align with God's Word, your conscience becomes more in tune with Him. But when you resist the truth or make sinful choices, your conscience dulls, distancing you from God (Hebrews 4:7).

This dulling effect is similar to how skin reacts to the sun. Over time, a sunbather's skin toughens and becomes leathery. Likewise, when you ignore or resist God's truth, your conscience hardens (1 Timothy 4:2). Eventually, this leads to spiritual blindness, where you no longer discern right from wrong—a dangerous place to be.

Biblical Voice Training

The goal is for your conscience and God's Word to "sing in harmony." When your inner voice aligns with Scripture, you'll experience true freedom and clarity for all of your decisions. To keep your conscience clear, you need to train it using the means of grace God provides.

1. **CANON (GOD'S WORD):** God's Word is the ultimate standard of truth. Regularly reading and meditating on Scripture will help you calibrate your conscience to God's will.

2. **COMFORTER (HOLY SPIRIT):** The Holy Spirit illuminates Scripture and convicts you of sin. Ask Him to guide your understanding and help you apply God's truth to your life so you do not quench or grieve Him.

3. **COMMUNITY (BIBLICAL FRIENDS):** Accountability from wise, godly friends can help you see blind spots and make choices that honor the Lord. Surround yourself with people who encourage you to grow spiritually.

4. **CONSCIENCE (INNER VOICE):** Your conscience affirms you when you walk in truth and warns you when you stray. Listen to it, but ensure it's informed by Scripture and not personal feelings or cultural norms.

Time to Reflect

1. How would you describe your conscience? Is it weak, hard, dull, or biblically informed? Take time to honestly evaluate how your inner voice reacts to life's situations.
2. How are the four means of grace working in your life?
3. Describe your time in God's Word.
4. What does seeking the Spirit's guidance mean?
5. Who holds you accountable; how are they doing?
6. Rate your conscience from 1 to 10. 1 being hard and 10 being in tune with God's Word? What changes will you make?

If your conscience isn't fully aligned with God's Word, what steps can you take to strengthen it? Commit to consistent Bible reading and reflection. Pray for the Holy Spirit to reveal areas where you need to grow. Seek out a trusted mentor or friend for accountability. Don't let your conscience become calloused or disconnected from God's truth. Instead, train it to reflect His Word and experience the freedom and joy that come from walking in harmony with Him.

Let's live boldly, ensuring our consciences are a faithful guide, tuned to God's voice.

Day 21

Describe Your Friendships

One of the most influential aspects of your life is your friendships. The relationships you keep play a significant role in shaping who you are and how you grow in your relationship with God. Though you can do many things alone, sanctification is not one of those things. If you want to mature in Christ, you need mature friends who have the grace and courage to spur you on to love and good deeds (Hebrews 10:24-25).

> *Faithful are the wounds of a friend; profuse are the kisses of an enemy*
>
> (Proverbs 27:6)

Friendships That Point to God

The most important relationship in your life is with God, and your closest friendships should help you experience Him more deeply. A community of like-minded believers who encourage you to mature in Christ is a gift from on High. If your current friendships don't provide this kind of care and encouragement, it might be time to reconsider who you're spending the most time with and how they affect you.

While bad influences will corrupt your good morals (1 Corinthians 15:33), good friends can sharpen, shape, and strengthen you (Proverbs 27:17). Surrounding yourself with people who love God and want to glorify Him will help you grow spiritually and live a more rational and purposeful life.

Practical Questions to Deepen Friendships

Here are some questions you can use to strengthen your friendships. These conversation starters will help you and your friends be transparent about your walk with God and encourage each other to grow:

1. What has the Lord taught you lately, and how is it affecting your life positively?
2. How have you applied what He taught you to your life to have that positive impact? Be practical and specific.
3. What have you read or heard that is helping you in your walk with God? How is it helping you practically?
4. What specific areas are you struggling with, and how may I come alongside you to help?
5. How can I serve you in a particular area of your sanctification—something you want to mature in?
6. What are some ways in which you are leading your friends? What changes are you seeing in them?

These questions aren't meant to intimidate or judge your friends but to help you build relationships centered on Christ.

Time to Reflect

1. How do you characterize your closest relationships? Are they helping you grow in your faith, or are they pulling you away from God?
2. Will you use these practical questions to strengthen your friendships? Commit to starting deeper conversations with one or two friends this week.

Take time today to pray for your friends, asking God to show you where you need to grow as a friend and to guide you toward relationships that will encourage you in your walk with Him.

Let's live boldly, cultivating friendships that glorify God and help us mature in Christ.

Day 22

Disciple Your Parents

Today's focus is on a challenging but vital responsibility: discipling your parents. As a believer, you are called to disciple and evangelize those in your sphere of influence—and that includes your family. Being an adult means acting like an adult, which expects you to come alongside other adults, helping them in their relationship with God. To love God and love others as you love yourself implies caring well for all people, even those who have had authority over you.

> When I was a child, I spoke like a child, I thought like a child, I reasoned like a child. When I became a man, I gave up childish ways.
>
> (1 Corinthians 13:11)

Your Ministry Starts at Home

Your ministry doesn't begin when you move out of your childhood home or start your own life. It begins now, within your family. Loving others as Christ loves you includes the individuals closest to you, like your siblings and parents. As a child, you primarily received care from your parents or guardians.

But as you grow, your role within the family shifts. Maturing spiritually means stepping into a caregiver's role, not only physically but also spiritually.

Honoring Your Parents Through Discipleship

Honoring your parents includes offering biblical care. This expectation might involve encouragement or correction, depending on the situation. Some people wrongly believe that correcting their parents is unloving, but the opposite is true. Lovingly pointing out a wayward path can be one of the most honoring and loving things you can do for anyone, including your parents.

Remember, discipleship isn't about criticism but care. When you lovingly correct or encourage your parents, you mirror God's love and care for you. This worldview is part of living out the gospel in your home.

Time to Reflect

1. Is it time for you to take your care to the next level? Reflect on your spiritual maturity.
2. Are you ready to disciple your parents with humility and love?
3. If so, what does discipling them mean, practically speaking?
4. What hinders you from bringing biblical care to your parents?
5. Are you afraid of their reaction?
6. Do you believe you are inadequate? Pray, asking God to give you the wisdom and courage to step into this role.

Practical Steps

1. Begin by praying for your parents daily. Ask God to work in their hearts and give you opportunities to encourage or guide them.
2. Look for ways to serve them practically, demonstrating Christ's love through your actions.
3. When correction is necessary, approach them with humility and respect, focusing on God's truth rather than your preferences.

Take time today to evaluate your relationship with your parents. Ask God to help you love them well, both in encouragement and correction, as you step into this maturing role.

Let's live boldly, embracing our calling to disciple and honor our parents in Christ-like love.

Day 23

The First Step Before You Start

An essential first step in discipleship is how you view others. If your disappointment in people is greater than your desire to help them, your ability to disciple effectively will run into many hindrances. Jesus had some strong language for those who made the log/speck mistake.

> Why do you see the speck that is in your brother's eye, but do not notice the log that is in your own eye? Or how can you say to your brother, "Let me take the speck out of your eye," when there is the log in your own eye? You hypocrite, first take the log out of your own eye, and then you will see clearly to take the speck out of your brother's eye.
>
> (Matthew 7:3-5)

The Importance of Perspective

How you think about others shapes the quality of the care you will provide. Jesus used the analogy of the log and speck in our eyes to highlight the importance of humility in relationships. Before helping someone with whatever their struggle may be, you must address your sin adequately.

This worldview isn't just a metaphor; it's a heart check. Discipleship flows best from a place of humility, where you see yourself as a fellow traveler on the path to becoming like Christ, not as someone who has arrived, and you're waiting for others to get to where you are.

Diagnostic Questions for Soul Care

Perhaps these questions will help you to assess your readiness for discipleship:

1. Do you consider yourself better than the person who needs your input? If so, pride may be clouding your ability to offer genuine care, and you must descend from your lofty perch so you might serve them.
2. Does your care for family members or friends feel like looking down on them? If your tone or attitude comes across as condescending, it can hurt the relationship and your witness.
3. Are you impatient with those who have yet to arrive where you are spiritually? Remember that growth takes time, and everyone's journey is different. Patience and grace are essential.

The person who views themself as a servant of all is best positioned to help others grow. Jesus modeled this servant-heartedness perfectly, and we are called to follow His example (Mark 10:45). The practical question that I am asking you is, "Who is the biggest sinner in the room?" If you do not see yourself as the foremost sinner—like the great apostle—I recommend you work on your heart first before you address others (1 Timothy 1:15-16).

Time to Reflect

1. Are you more controlled by God's call to disciple others or by people's actions toward you? If people's failures frustrate you, refocus on God's call to serve them.

2. What specific way do you need to change regarding the "log and speck" paradigm? Identify an area where pride might be hindering your ability to care for others well.

Practical Steps

1. Spend time in prayer, asking God to reveal any logs in your life that need attention.
1. Practice humility by reminding yourself that you, too, are in need of grace daily.
2. When discipling others, focus on encouragement and truth rather than criticism or judgment.

Discipleship is a beautiful but challenging calling. It requires humility, patience, and a servant's heart. As you grow in these qualities, you'll be better equipped to walk alongside others in their journey toward Christ.

Let's live boldly, humbly aligning our hearts with God's call to love and disciple well.

Day 24

How to Make a Decision

M any people struggle with decision-making. The most crucial question you can ask yourself when making a decision is this: Am I in faith to do this? In other words, do you believe that what you're considering is the right thing to do? Are you sure? Is this God's will? Is your faith greater than your doubts?

> But whoever has doubts is condemned if he eats, because the eating is not from faith. For whatever does not proceed from faith is sin.
>
> (Romans 14:23)

Faith as a Stool

Faith is like a four-legged stool. To be in faith about a decision, the stool must be balanced and stable. The four legs represent the four means of grace God provides to guide you through the decision-making process:

- **CANON (GOD'S WORD):** What does the Bible say about your decision? Scripture is your ultimate authority and should be your first stop when seeking wisdom (2 Timothy 3:16-17).
- **COMMUNITY (WISE FRIENDS):** What do trusted, courageous, and wise friends say? Seek advice from

people who love God and want the best for you (Proverbs 11:14).

- **CONSCIENCE (INNER VOICE):** What does your conscience tell you? Your inner voice, when informed by Scripture and humility, will guide you biblically (Romans 2:14-15).
- **COMFORTER (HOLY SPIRIT):** What does the Spirit of God say? The Holy Spirit leads and illuminates truth (John 16:13). Take time to pray for and discern His guidance.

The Danger of Neglect

Most poor decisions occur when someone neglects one or more of these means of grace. Sometimes, this happens out of ignorance, but other times, it might be because of stubbornness or other forms of pride. Humility is essential in decision-making. Hold your ideas loosely, submit them to God's Word, and seek input from His community.

Time to Reflect

1. Which of the four means of grace is your most significant struggle?
2. Do you neglect Scripture when making decisions?
3. Are you hesitant to seek advice from others?
4. Do you struggle to trust your conscience?
5. Do you need help discerning the Holy Spirit's leading?
6. What is your plan to change any potential inadequacies in the decision-making process?
7. If you struggle with the Canon, commit to regular Bible reading and study.
8. If you avoid Community, ask a trusted mentor or friend to walk alongside you in your decision-making process.
9. If your Conscience seems unclear, pray for God to

align your heart with His truth.

10. If you need clarification on the Comforter, spend more time in prayer, asking the Holy Spirit for clarity and peace.

Practical Application

Before making your next decision, evaluate it using all four legs of the decision-making stool. Write down what Scripture says, seek advice from wise friends, examine your conscience, and pray for the Spirit's guidance.

Let's live boldly, making decisions that honor God and reflect faith grounded in His grace.

Day 25

Sex Before Marriage

Today's focus is a sensitive but vital topic: sex before marriage. God's design for physical intimacy is within the context of marriage, and stepping outside that design can lead to long-lasting consequences in your spiritual, emotional, and relational life (Hebrews 13:4).

> For this is the will of God, your sanctification: that you abstain from sexual immorality; that each one of you know how to control his own body in holiness and honor, not in the passion of lust like the Gentiles who do not know God.
>
> (1 Thessalonians 4:3-5)

Why Purity Matters

Many couples who come to marriage counseling have had sex before marriage. While this isn't always the root of their problems, it often creates unresolved issues that resurface in their relationship after they tie the knot. Sin has a way of compounding itself, creating patterns that harden consciences, damage relationships, and hinder spiritual growth. Sometimes, you don't know the origins until decades later.

The way someone lives today is a preview of how they will live in their marriage—either for better or worse. A partner walking in the Spirit will continue to grow in grace, while one walking in the flesh will likely grow further from God. Don't deceive yourself into thinking you or your relationship is the exception to this rule.

Seek Wise Counsel

If you need clarification on your relationship or your partner's spiritual walk, seek God-centered counsel from a trusted mentor or biblical leader. This need is not about checking a box but engaging in a divine appointment where you can learn, grow, and make necessary changes.

The Side Effects of Sexual Sin

Allowing sin to go unchecked has serious consequences. Let me provide a few examples:

1. **HARDENED CONSCIENCE:** Ignoring God's convictions dulls your sensitivity to the Spirit.
2. **DYSFUNCTIONAL RELATIONSHIPS:** Sin introduces patterns of mistrust, guilt, and unresolved conflict.
3. **DISPLEASURE TO GOD:** The Lord desires your holiness, making Him a warring army against pride (James 4:6).

God gave you a conscience as a kindness, alerting you to sin and calling you to respond biblically. Ignoring that call hardens your heart, steals your joy, and damages your ability to build healthy relationships.

Time to Reflect

1. Have you had sex before marriage? If so, have you confessed this sin to God and sought His forgiveness?
2. What are you doing to stay morally pure?

3. Will you confide in a trusted biblical mentor about your plans to stay pure?

Practical Steps

1. **SET BORDERS:** Establish clear limits in your relationships to honor God and protect your purity.
2. **CONFESS AND REPENT:** If you've fallen into sexual sin, confess it to God and seek His forgiveness. Consider talking to a mentor for guidance and accountability.
3. **PRAY FOR STRENGTH:** Ask God for the strength to resist temptation and the wisdom to glorify Him.

God's design for sex is not about restricting you but about protecting you and helping you flourish in a marriage centered on Him. Honor Him now by pursuing purity, trusting that His plan is always for your good.

Let's live boldly, living in the freedom and joy of God's design for our lives.

Day 26

Managed by Opinions

Overcoming the fear of others disapproval is a universal struggle for those who base their identity on what others think of them. When we act like this, we give others power over us. We're nothing more than puppets on a string, always managed by the fickle approval of others. The Bible calls this the fear of man, but you might recognize it better as peer pressure, codependency, or insecurity.

> The fear of man lays a snare, but whoever trusts in the LORD is safe.
>
> (Proverbs 29:25)

The Fear of Man

It's natural to want acceptance and approval from others, but when that desire controls you, it becomes sin. Insecure people often ask questions like:

- Will they hurt me?
- Will they reject me?
- Will they like me?

Living under the weight of these queries trap you, but God extends freedom. As your faith grows, His opinion of you becomes more controlling than anyone else's.

Freedom Through the Gospel

When you're under the control of God's truth, you are no longer a victim managed by what you want from others. Instead of being shaped their acceptance, you rest in the truth of who God says you are. Here are three reasons why you can be secure in God's opinion of you:

- **IT'S POSITIVE:** Your sins are forgiven. The righteousness of Christ covers you. God sees you as His beloved child.
- **IT'S UNCHANGING:** God's love for you is steadfast and eternal—unlike shifting human acceptance.
- **IT'S SATISFYING:** God's approval brings a deep, unshakable peace that no human opinion can match.

Read Romans 8:31-39 to remind yourself of the security you have in God's love.

Your Choice

You get to choose who or what controls your mind:

- **FEAR OF MAN:** Allowing other people's opinions to dictate your thoughts and actions.
- **FEAR OF GOD:** Resting in the truth that God's love for you is greater than any human opinion.

Submitting yourself to God is the only way to experience true maturity and freedom.

Time to Reflect

1. Are you a Christian? How do you know? Take time to reflect on your relationship with God. If you're unsure, consider what it means to trust Jesus.
2. How is God's opinion managing you? Are you more influenced by Him or by what others think? What practical steps must you take to find security in the gospel? Here are some suggestions:
3. Read daily, meditating on Scripture, particularly about God's love and promises.
4. Pray for God to strengthen your faith and help you let go of the need for human approval.
5. Surround yourself with friends who encourage you to live for God's glory rather than people's opinions.

Rest in the truth of the gospel. God's opinion of you is the only opinion that truly matters, and His love is more satisfying and enduring than any human approval.

Let's live boldly, choosing to live for God's glory rather than the fleeting opinions of others.

Day 27

Self-reliance Is a Myth

Learning to overcome our all-time and number one problem and the cultural myth of self-reliance is vital for a robust Christian life. Self-sufficiency is a synonym for unbelief, choosing to rely on ourselves instead of the Lord. The truth is that no one can live completely independent of God—not even Jesus lived that way.

> For we do not want you to be unaware, brothers, of the affliction we experienced in Asia. For we were so utterly burdened beyond our strength that we despaired of life itself. Indeed, we felt that we had received the sentence of death. But that was to make us rely not on ourselves but on God who raises the dead.
>
> (2 Corinthians 1:8-9)

The Illusion of Self-Sufficiency

A self-reliant person lives in a fantasy world, imagining he can be in control without help from others. This mindset is isolating and deceiving. It projects an image of strength, but in reality, it reveals weakness and arrogance. Weakness because we're finite and arrogance because only a fool chooses self-reliance. Even Jesus resisted self-sufficiency. He chose to humble Himself to God's will, saying, "For I have come down from heaven, not to do My own will, but the will of Him who sent Me" (John 6:38). If the perfect Son of God acknowledged His dependence on the Father, how much more should we?

The Danger of Self-Reliance

Self-sufficiency is rooted in pride—a desire to avoid trusting God or accepting help from others. It's an attempt to control life on one's own terms. This mindset leads to relational complexities. God designed us to be dependent on Him and interdependent with each other. Pretending to be self-sufficient is a form of insanity. It denies the reality of our brokenness and our need for help. Apart from Him, we cannot do anything (John 15:5).

God-Dependency Is the Truth

Whether you admit it or not, you are dependent on God for every breath, every opportunity, and every ounce of strength. Recognizing this truth is the first step toward living a life of humility and freedom, which is found in relying on Him, who raises the dead. The world promotes self-reliance as a path to greatness, but true success is found in surrendering to God and allowing Him to guide and sustain you.

Time to Reflect

1. What specific ways do you struggle with self-reliance?
   - Do you resist asking for help when you need it?
   - Do you sense the need to appear strong and in control before others?
   - Are you hesitant to trust God fully with your decisions and future?

2. What is your practical plan to overcome this anti-God sin pattern? Here are a few suggestions.
   - **PRAY FOR HUMILITY:** Ask God to help you see your need for Him and to give you a dependent heart.
   - **SEEK WISE COUNSEL:** Surround yourself with people who encourage you to trust God and lean on others.
   - **TAKE SMALL STEPS:** Ask for help when you struggle. Trust God to work through your relationships.
   - **STUDY JESUS' EXAMPLE:** Reflect on John 6:38 to understand how Jesus depended on the Father.

Living a God-dependent life isn't a sign of weakness; it's a reflection of wisdom. Recognizing your need for God and others frees you to experience His grace and strength in every area of life.

Let's live boldly, letting go of the illusion of self-sufficiency and embracing the truth that God is our ultimate source of strength and provision.

Day 28

The Reason to Love

L et's talk about love—not the kind that looks like an empty love cup but the kind that reflects God's character by giving and serving in a way that glorifies Him. Love is a communicable attribute, a gift that God has communicated (given) to us. Thus, we can love well, but due to our fallenness, loving well can turn inward, self-focused, and distorted.

> For even the Son of Man came not to be served but to serve, and to give his life as a ransom for many.
> (Mark 10:45)

Love That Images the Trinity

Perhaps a few questions might help: Why do you want relationships? Why do you desire to date, marry, or be part of a community? The number one reason should not be about meeting your deepest longings or filling an emotional void. The ultimate purpose of relationships is to image the Trinity—Father, Son, and Spirit—in a relational community. The Trinity is the original Divine community, eternally loving and giving within itself. When God created Adam, He designed him to reflect this relational nature. Adam was made in God's image and could display God's character—His holiness, love, patience, wisdom, and more.

The Problem of Aloneness

However, Adam was alone, and God declared, "It is not good for man to be alone" (Genesis 2:18). Adam didn't lack someone to fill his proverbial love cup but needed someone to share a relational community where the fullness of God's image could be displayed.

In this sense, Adam was like a star athlete without a team—ready and equipped but without an outlet to fulfill his purpose. Eve was created not simply to satisfy Adam's needs but to partner with him in reflecting God's relational nature to the world.

Love That Gives, Not Demands

True love seeks to give, not to take. Love is active, always moving from the giver to the receiver. The self-absorbed and self-indulgent has one aim: to receive love. It's called self-love where all the action flows back to the self-centered soul. If you want to be happy and whole, you must find your fullness by serving others rather than demanding they meet your needs. The fullest people you will ever meet are those who pour their lives into others.

Jesus exemplified this perfectly. Wherever He went, He put the Father on display by loving, serving, and helping others. By pouring Himself into others, Jesus imaged a God-designed community. You are called to do the same. Rather than asking, "How can people make me feel better?" ask, "How can I reflect God by loving and serving the people around me?" It's counterintuitive to the instincts of the culture, but if you want to experience the love of God and others to the fullest, practice loving God and others as you love yourself.

Time to Reflect

1. Do you need people to make you feel better, or do you need people to display the many aspects of the Father, Son, and Spirit? Reflect on your motivations for relationships. Are you seeking to receive or to give primarily?
2. What is one way you can change to be a better lover, server, and helper of people? Consider one practical step you can take today to love others selflessly. This action might include acts of kindness, offering encouragement, or simply listening with patience and care.

Relationships aren't primarily about what you can gain but about how you can glorify God by reflecting His love and character. Start today by looking for ways to serve and uplift others, just as Christ did.

Let's live boldly, loving others well and imaging the Trinity in every relationship.

Day 29

Re-evaluating Self-Esteem

I want to re-evaluate a prior devotion and rethink the cultural message of self-esteem. While the world tells you to focus on yourself to find freedom, the Bible teaches a counterintuitive truth: the path to freedom is found in thinking less about yourself and more about God and others.

> Do nothing from selfish ambition or conceit, but in humility count others more significant than yourselves. Let each of you look not only to his own interests, but also to the interests of others.
> (Philippians 2:3-4)

The Problem with Self-Esteem

The self-esteem agenda calls you to admire and focus on yourself. It claims to be the solution for struggles like guilt, shame, fear, or insecurity. But this unbiblical concept often leads to more pain and disillusionment. Why? Turning your thoughts inward only magnifies and amplifies the darkness in your soul. Looking inward is not the solution. The more our gaze goes upward, the freer we will become.

From a biblical perspective, low self-esteem isn't the real problem, and elevating self-admiration isn't the solution. Thinking more about yourself—whether to inflate your ego or cure your insecurities—only deepens your self-centeredness.

The Bible is clear: apart from God's grace, we are all hopeless and sinful (Romans 3:10-12). Looking inward for solutions blinds us to the only real hope—Jesus Christ.

The Gospel's Counterintuitive Message

Jesus didn't come to help you focus on yourself; He came to rescue you from yourself. He came to clothe you in His righteousness, freeing you from the burden of self-centered thinking (John 8:36). The gospel declares that our depravity is the perfect backdrop for God's redemptive work.

When you stop trying to elevate your self-worth and instead focus on the worth of Christ, you experience true freedom. The more you turn your thoughts to God and others, the freer and more joyful you become.

Time to Reflect

1. Have you succumbed to self-centered thinking? Are you trapped in inward-focused thoughts, whether they center on guilt, insecurity, or self-admiration? If so, the solution is not to look deeper into yourself but to lift your eyes to Jesus.
2. How does God's salvation free you from introspection? Reflect on how God's grace releases you from the exhausting cycle of self-focus. His salvation clothes you in Christ's righteousness, empowering you to love Him and serve others.

Practical Steps to Shift Your Focus

*   **MEDITATE ON SCRIPTURE:** Spend time in passages like Romans 3:10-24 and Philippians 2:3-4, which highlight the sufficiency of Christ and the call to humility.
*   **PRAY FOR OTHERS:** Shift your thoughts outward by interceding for the needs of others.

- **SERVE IN LOVE:** Look for opportunities to serve someone this week, reflecting Christ's love instead of focusing on yourself.

True freedom isn't found in self-esteem but in Christ-esteem. The gospel frees you from the exhausting task of focusing on yourself and releases you to love God and others well.

Let's live boldly, embracing the gospel's counterintuitive message and finding freedom in Christ.

Day 30

Your Secret Weapon

L et's uncover and discover one of the most powerful tools God has given you for growth: repentance. The typical Christian understands repentance as something that happens at salvation, but its role in sanctification—your ongoing transformation—is often overlooked. The Christian life is repentance at salvation and ongoing repenting in our progressive sanctification.

> To put off your old self, which belongs to your former manner of life and is corrupt through deceitful desires, and to be renewed in the spirit of your minds, and to put on the new self, created after the likeness of God in true righteousness and holiness.
> (Ephesians 4:22-24)

The Purpose of Repentance

Repentance is the Bible's word for change, and it's the reason Jesus came to earth. While salvation secures our relationship with God, ongoing repenting transforms our life day by day. It's the process of becoming more like Christ—what we call progressive sanctification.

Think of your spiritual growth like your physical growth. When you were born, you weren't fully developed; you had years of growth in the future to become mature. Similarly, being born again is just the starting point. The rest of your life is about learning, growing, transforming, and maturing into Christlikeness (1 Peter 2:2).

Distinguishing Salvation and Sanctification

SALVATION:
- Secures your justification—declared not guilty
- Adopts you into God's family
- Guarantees your eternal future

SANCTIFICATION:
- Prepares you to live well in a fallen world
- Helps you overcome sin and reflect Christ's character
- Is an ongoing process of growth and change

Salvation happens in a moment; sanctification occurs over a lifetime. You don't need to be born again twice, but you do need to keep repenting, learning, and transforming.

How to Repent

Repentance isn't about saying sorry; it's about realigning your thoughts, desires, and actions with God's Word. Here's a simple framework for repentance:

1. **IDENTIFY THE SIN:** Be honest about the specific area in your life that doesn't align with God's standards.
2. **CONFESS IT TO GOD:** Acknowledge your sin and ask for forgiveness (1 John 1:9).
3. **SEEK ACCOUNTABILITY:** Share your struggle with a trusted Christian friend or mentor who can guide and encourage you.
4. **TAKE ACTION:** Make practical changes to turn away from sin and toward Christ.

Time to Reflect

1. What is one thing about you that you want to change? Take time to reflect on an area of your life where you need transformation.
2. Will you share that with a compassionate Christian mentor? Seek someone competent, courageous, and compassionate to walk with you through the process of repentance.

Repentance isn't just a one-time event; it's a lifelong journey of becoming more like Jesus. Embrace it as your secret weapon for growth, and watch how God transforms your life for His glory.

Let's live boldly, committing to a life of ongoing repentance and Christlike transformation.

Day 31

Whatever You Do, Do This

As we conclude this series, we will focus on the most crucial aspect of your life—the one thing that should shape every decision, every action, and every relationship. The question is simple and yet it is profound: What is your ultimate motive for all you do in life? Perhaps you could think of it as a mission statement. Listen to the great apostle.

> So, whether you eat or drink, or whatever you do, do all to the glory of God.
>
> (1 Corinthians 10:31)

What Will They Say About You?

Think about how you'd like to be remembered after you die. What would you want others to say about your life? My question isn't meant to make you morbid but to help you identify your highest priority. Whatever your answer is, it will serve as the lens through which you view life and make decisions. The good news is that God has already revealed what your ultimate aim should be—to live for His glory.

God's Glory: Your Chief Aim

For Paul, glorifying God was the transcendent goal that shaped everything he did. No pursuit was more important to him than making God's name great and spreading His fame. To glorify God means:

- Honoring Him as the center of your life.
- Spreading His fame in all you do.
- Living in holy awe of who He is and letting that awe guide your decisions.

Whether in small tasks—eating and drinking, or in the more significant life goals like marriage, children, career—God's glory should be your driving purpose.

Eternal Perspective

One day, everyone—both in heaven and hell—will glorify God for eternity (Philippians 2:9-11). But glorifying Him now, in your daily life, is your opportunity to live with purpose, focus, and joy. The weight of God's worth—His glory—gives your life its ultimate meaning.

Time to Reflect

1. Do you see the importance of God's glory as your chief aim? Take a moment to evaluate your daily life. Are your decisions, relationships, and goals driven by a desire to honor God?
2. What does glorifying God look like practically?
   - **IN YOUR RELATIONSHIPS:** Show kindness, humility, and patience, reflecting God's love for others.
   - **IN YOUR WORK OR SCHOOL:** Do your tasks with excellence and integrity; you represent Christ.
   - **IN YOUR FREE TIME:** Use your time to serve others, grow in your faith, and avoid distractions that pull you away from God.

Living for God's glory is not just a lofty ideal; it's a practical, daily commitment. Start small—invite God into your everyday activities and ask Him to help you align your thoughts, words, and actions with His purpose.

Let's live boldly, living every day to the glory of God, making His name great in all the earth.

Conclusion

Congratulations! You've completed this 31-day devotional journey. Over the past month—or whatever your pace has been—you've explored biblical truths that challenge cultural norms, deepen your faith, and equip you for life's daily battles.

But this isn't the end—it's just the beginning. The insights you've gained and the truths you've embraced are meant to fuel a lifetime of growth in Christ. Every day, you have the opportunity to glorify God in the ordinary as well as the extraordinary, to reflect His love in your relationships, and to make choices that honor Him.

As you move forward, remember that God is with you. His grace is sufficient, His Word is your guide, and His Spirit empowers you. Continue to seek Him, trust Him, and live for His glory. Share what you've learned with others, and invite them to walk this journey of faith alongside you.

Perhaps going through this devotional yearly would prove beneficial. You probably figured out that a devotion for young adults might not be the best title. The truths I have presented to you apply to any Christian, regardless of their age. Consider sharing these ideas with your friends—regardless of their age. Perhaps a 31-day challenge in person or online could ignite many lives for Christ.

The Lord has incredible plans for your life—plans to use you for His glory and your good. Keep pressing into Him, and watch how He transforms your life into something more beautiful than you could ever imagine.

Let's live boldly together, fully committed to making God the center of everything we think, say, and do.

To God be the glory,

Rick

About the Author

Rick Thomas launched the Life Over Coffee global training network in 2008 to bring hope and help for you and others by creating resources that spark conversations for transformation. His primary responsibilities are resource creation and leadership development, which he does through speaking, writing, podcasting, and educating. In 1990 he earned a BA in Theology and, in 1991, a BS in Education. In 1993, he received his ordination into Christian ministry, and in 2000, he graduated with an MA in Counseling from The Master's University. In 2006, he was recognized as a Fellow of the Association of Certified Biblical Counselors (ACBC).

Other Books Available from Life Over Coffee

Boasting in Weakness
Centering Your Marriage on Christ
Communication
Complete Marriage
Don't Apologize
Exchange the Truth for a Lie
Help My Marriage Has Grown Cold
Identity Crisis
Local Church
Loving Me
Mad
Marriage Devotion We Are One
Politics and Culture
Parenting Devotion from Zero to Adulthood
Sex, Temptation, and Modesty
Storm Hurler
The Cyber Effect
The Talk
Wives Leading
You Decide